POEMS FROM A HOUSE OF GLASS

: I :

The Fledgling Spirit Flies

POEMS FROM A HOUSE OF GLASS

: I :

The Fledgling Spirit Flies

by F. B. Cornell

Vantage Press
NEW YORK

～ Contents ～

A VOYAGE

PARAGRAPHS

Foreword

I dwelt innocent years in Time's house of stone,
Unwindowed, with mirrors set all around;
I wondered somewhat to live so alone.

But by that long mirroring there of me
I finally dared myself truly to see
And then endure. Now, at last set free

From mirrors and stone, I am able to pass
Across an open and untrammeled space
To dwell in this many-roomed House of Glass.

DAYS OF INNOCENCE

The search for its direction
within the young body and the mind
by an awakening spirit

Evening Rain

A light from across the street
Explodes through rain
In stars ejaculated
Against a rigid sky.
The flickering
Of its pool-deepened eye
Spits fire against water drops.
Rays lance out, extinguish,
Then leap forth again
To rend the rain and darkness
With excruciating flame.

From each incontinent shaft of light
Bright daggers rip
To tear the womb of night,
Suggest some reminiscent pain,
Agony endured from ancient flight
When each was kindled from a greater light,
Flame wrenched from mightier flame.

Lonely separated sparks
Of multiplication endured,
They pierce the slanting rain and night,
Frantic scintillating light
Hurled outward
Slashing at the rain.

Each spark in fury strives again
To dissipate the vaporous dark
That damps its burning;
Each, self-consumed by longing
For single light, for prior flame;
Condemned to the tragedy of flight
Out to extinction through the night;
Whose wildest rapture
Longs only for returning.

Rain ends and a light burns on
In the window across the street,
Pure and clear and strong.
Above the soaking lawn
Darkness heals itself, grows again complete,
No longer torn
By illusions of out-flying sparks.
All is tranquil; agony has gone.
Light disappears as a hand is lifted
And a window shade is drawn.

Among the Pictures from the Past

She plays the piano absently as though to prolong
The dusk; the scent of moss roses in June; the circus train
Hoots anticipation into a midnight town;
They drive all day through pine forests isinglassed with rain;

Toys are kept in a cupboard under the stairs;
Freshly laundered curtains dry on a frame. Absence
Is a window looking toward the end of an empty street;
Like various drawings these — portrait, still life, scene,

Even doodles carefully preserved to assuage memory,
To line its passageways, crowd corridors, closed rooms.
Yet nowhere can I experience, search as I will,
Through hours spent in longing's galleried space

The excitement always shining on me from her eyes
Or the glow of expectation lighting up my face.

Dormitory — At a College Recess

They all have gone
And tight-locked doors
Conceal the things which stand for them,
The symbols of their having been:
Clothes, a book, a broken pen
And papers roughly scribbled o'er —
All hidden by a staring door.

The corridors
Where late they walked
Are poised in silence, all at rest,
And only little winds like sighs
Murmur against the walls, suggest,
Beyond all power of eye to see,
Some absence of their company.

Shadows of laughter
Cling within
Hallways leading me to sleep,
Within the darkness echoed-words
An ebbing vigil seem to keep.
Ghosts of gay expectancy move
Through the rooms above my head,
And every time I shut my eyes
Sharp night sounds of departure arise
To troop my tumbled bed.

Winter Awakening

Lurid fingerings of the dawn
Scratch their streaks above the town,
The sun reluctantly comes to fire
On barn and dwelling, roof and spire.

Crimson spreads and splotches snow
Mottled still with shapes of night,
Shadows that hide from a day's advance
Resist its crude attack of light.

Three trees stand, stark and black,
As hanged men painted on orange glass
Which rises into an eastern sky;
A day of winter begins and I,

Night-numbed, must all too soon
Cast oblivion's coverlet aside
And struggle to resume.

Wayfarer

I stood at the door
And watched him come
Across bare fields
Against a sun.
A wrinkled god
Driven from home,
He had wandered far,
Ancient, alone.
He bore as token
Within his hand
A flowering branch.
"Plant this," he said,
And died at my feet.

I buried them deep,
The god and the branch,
In winter earth
That there might be born
From their grave in the spring
A flowering thorn,
That flourishing it
Might divinely bear
A blossoming limb
For my wandering year.

Now I must go,

Mere man, to roam
Humbly the world,
A searcher, alone,
Hoping to find
One who can share
The heavy branch
Of love I bear.

There Shall Be Two

The Minotaur, the Unicorn
Were assigned when time began
To endure in combat,
Fracture Promethean;

Joined by contradiction's nerve
In war by death unmarred,
Denied reprieve of sunset,
No dawn unsanguine scarred,

Bound to impossibly expiate
The curse of myths opposed,
Immortally healed to conflict
From every mortal wound;

Behemoth this, the other sleek,
A mouth of vilest breath
Attack'd by horn of silver,
Made two in one contest.

The Minotaur, the Unicorn
In pastures dark beyond mind
Graze together amiably
As undifferenced as two kine.

Images

1. Autumn Afternoon

White cloud boats lean their regattas overhead
While I, entangled in the mystery of my seaweed trees
Whose branches wave in currents of the wind,
Look up to see, swim there
Within October tides of day,
Seeking with bulging eyes and finny motions to assay
The secret of these competitions of the sky;
Wonder if the whitest keel will win,
Who steers, and why a breeze
Should seek to favor him.
Discover when all the clouds have sailed away
That emptiness remains
And boats were only piscine absurdity
For all their hurrah of pennants,
Singing ropes and scudding wakes;
Acts of a supreme fragility
Which leave no impress on this element,
Indispensable blue medium of me,
Where I continue to be
Myself, a sinuous wondering;
Immersed and laved
By afternoon currents of eternity.

2. *Pasture*

It rains;
And yet the cattle on the hill
Are as unconcerned
As though a day were still
Patterned with sun;
Undisturbed, the strung-out herd
Grazes gray meadow,
Heads all bent
To wild-hay grasses of contentment
Until they pass
Beyond a knoll of birch.
The thin calf frisks its heels
In an awkward lurch
After its cow;
Sloping pastureland
Lies shadowless and prone
Under opening clouds,
Empty now
Of all meaning save its own,
Luminousness
Peculiar to neither rain nor sun.

3. Shopping Center: Night

Porphyry tabernacles line the way
Displaying girdles, watches,
Hot cross buns on altars,
In velvet-covered trays wedding bands
Conceived of stainless steel. Concrete fountains
Multiply neon suns strung above arcades
To illuminate, as false teeth might a face,
Store fronts. Protoplasmic eyes in currents of glass
Like sea-jellies linked in copulative pairs
Exude their drops upon (from valves opened to seize)
Shoes and necklaces, underwear, overcoats,
Canned peas; eyes without noses, minus faces,
Freed of bodies, drifting reliquaries
Whose holy tears slide down no cheeks:
Phylogenic eons peer from seaweed forests
Into grottoes of anemone merchandise;
Among them everywhere, like gentle winds
Fingering fish scales in a gutter,
Eddies of desire sigh;
All around the parking lot
The newly planted little trees
Submit to unnatural overtures of spotlights
Upon their leaves.

4. Summer Scene

A grass stalk trembles;
The bee tumbles from its flower
To angle wing against lengthening shadow.
Willows by the barn
Turn down green-golden streams,
Extend earth-reflected branches
Slowly across a creek.
A certain sheen of light
Descends upon the marsh.
From my front steps I watch
Someone who walks along the road
(But I forget to care
Whether it is anyone I need to know or not).
All this what I
Engrave upon a waxen afternoon
With the stylus of awakened insight,
Engross a Country Scene, Contentment, Eventide.
Should I close my eyes
Nothing will have been
Except for a little chord, refined from emptiness,
Born within my ear
From a hieroglyph that vibrates in my mind.

5. *Arrival of Winter*

Cloud lions leap upon the world
And paralyze streams with icy tongues
Until a frail whip of snow uncurls
To drive them back for a day or two
Behind frost-blackened bars of hills.
On a morning not long thereafter
Going out I find to my horror
Blood and pigeon feather
Frozen on brittle emerald green.
The beasts have escaped, come back again.

I replenish my fire when I go in,
Count over my seeds, labeled and stored,
String some like a rosary on a cord;
Turn sprouting roots on a cellar floor;
Then in fitfully smoking lamplight sit
And thumb through old collected almanacs.
The cracked record on the gramophone
Muffles the sound of eager tongues
That lick hungrily at the door.

6. *City After Rain*

The sunken city
Is full of sound again
Now that a wind
Has carried off the rain.
In wet streets
People come and go;
A dark woman leans
From a high window;
The sound of dancing
Pours from an open door;
A blind is lowered
On the next floor.

Water stands in puddles
On the street
Jeweled by light.
A man, seeking
But discreet,
Stares at a woman
Who walks where pavements gleam
Bright as dark glass
Sunk in a stream.

The soiled city ways
After evening rain

Shimmer with wetness,
Washed clean, washed clean!

7. *Winter Nocturne*

Snowflakes falter in the air,
Slowly spiral down,
Soften angles of tree and house;
Bare backyards are lost, woodpile and barn,
As winter drifts in to fill
The streets and alleys of the town.

Ribbons of light unfurl
Across a temporary evening sky;
Fires of day die down;
The ghostly glow of sun is gone,
The chill of night comes on.

And I, hurrying toward home,
The only thing that moves,
Stride hunched with collar upturned,
Across the lavender close
Of mid-winter afternoon —

Eager to escape the deft and inconclusive touch
Of cold upon my hands and mouth;
Eager to attain the reassurance of my room,
Radiatored and lamplit cubicle
Stagnant with warmth.

8. *Allegro*

Certainly spring must come at last;
In a sun-warmed areaway I passed
Three little girls at play,
Sheltered from raw March blast;

Skipping rope, three shrill-voic'd maids,
Firm cheeks flushed and bouncing braids;
Outer garments were cast away;
Everywhere laughter sprayed.

What ancient cold can foil virgin joy,
Fecundity ripe and no longer coy?
It was still a blustering day
But caresses warmed my face.

Seascape

Gulls wheel from remote cloud arches,
This secret beach invade
Where I cast passionate nakedness
Into the hands of wave.

Gulls shatter with flight the seascape,
White-pierce sky's turquoise height.
Gulls plunge! The sea foam shatters
Into ejected light.

Gulls enter the distance. Horizon
Seals spent afternoon of sky,
And I, inert by the seaside, recall
Gulls' bitter, womanish cry.

An Appreciation

My father was an amiable man
    Who played at golf the eighteen holes,
Showered and came at one o'clock
    To carve a Sunday-dinner roast.

He took an early suburban train
    Each morning to executive desk,
Retired every evening at ten
    And lay beside his wife in rest.

His lawns were clipped, his fireplace bright,
    A dec'rous Packard his automobile;
He bought tuberculosis stamps
    And hated Roosevelt as the Devil.

He sent me to an Eastern school
    And praised my grades in composition,
Called me son, sent checks and came
    To admire cum laude graduation;

Saw me established in a place
    Where future advancement was assured
And advised me on the ways a man
    By his companions moves moneyward.

At eighty he took me to his club
　　For weekly lunch of comradeship
And shyly pressed my hand at parting
　　As thanks for my companionship.

My father was an amiable man
　　Who would have been appalled by genius;
I wish I might have someway found
　　A means of communication between us.

In Memoriam

This is his terror:
The clay-colored worm
That twists beneath his door
And inches toward him
Across the bare boards of the floor.

The white eye of the moon
Has turned opaque with horror
And presses its stare
Against the window of the cabin.

This is his soft terror:
It crawls into the firelight,
Steals away the heat,
Extinguishes the lamp,
Mounts his stiffening limbs
With a contracting grip
Measured by the ticking of the clock.

Tick tock!   Tick tock!   Tick tock!

His most secret being:
Paralyzed by an ecstasy of self-abandonment
Awaits, where it has fled
Into the most remote corner of his existence,
The exquisite pleasures of martyrdom.

Bird-in-a-Cage

This Time's a Cage
Confines the Bird of Being's flight,
Taming his freedom to alight
Upon Life's perch set sure and straight
Across a corner of Eternity
There to flutter and chirp and mate.

Around him are ranged the tensile bars
Of a silver-sheened Reality
To mark off intervals magically
Of Minutes, Hours, Days and Years
Until to his observation appears
Consistency, a world contrived,
Whose limiting circle stays his eye
Until it becomes his habit to see
Measured distance exclusively,
Dimensions of Thought clearly defined,
Narrowed, by Reason clearly defined,
A Universe grown cylindrical
Wherein he dwells and turns his face
Away from the Bright Beyond he knew,
Denies Realmlessness from whence he flew.

Caught in the cage he learns to sing,
To sit upon his perch and preen,

To cock his head from side to side,
Admire his own bright-feathered sheen.

He stretches forth an emerald wing
To hide his head when he would sleep
And in sleep's depth alone he sees
The timelessness where he might glide
Within an infinite airy stream,
Fly blissfully his way across
A spacelessness beyond his thought.

When he awakes the vision dissolves
Into foolish impossibles;
He chirps and preens and sings some more
And takes his seed. By chance his door
Is left ajar, in rare alarm
He cocks his head
And droops and scolds nor flies afar,
But sits and trembles and chirps instead.

Entranced, Bright Bird, by silver wires
Set evenly around his cage,
Bound to a flickering passage of hours
He must acquiesce to a cage's fate.
His will has been tamed not to aspire
Beyond world's brightness, such safe image.

Once Wondrous Bird, if he but knew
What thing he was before he flew

Into this tiny space of cage,
What limitless freedoms he then spanned,
What heavenly currents he engaged,
He would sit and weep for all he had been.

Behold! Time's wires, by tears dissolved,
Would disappear and, lancing forth,
What he now can't imagine, again he would be,
Rapt creature soaring upon a wing
Indistinguishable from supporting wind.

In life only danger he now recalls
In visions thrilled by the lift and fall
Of miraculous currents of ecstasy
Wherein, divinely, he once flew free!
How little he knows
Of splendored hurricanes, storms which blow
And stream around the dimensional space
Where he busily hops within his cage.
He assumes life's portion for his pattern,
Chirps and preens and mates and peers;
He becomes a pet, of all passion barren,
Self-indulged to grief and fear;
Hypnotized by water and seed
He makes a virtue of his greed,
Withholds sweet tears of aspiration
And flutters and chirps and sings and breeds.
At last swelled fat and proudly old

He falls stone dead upon his floor,
There to lie still securely bound
By death as in life closely around.

Whether to Heaven or Hell you fly,
Poor bird, bright bars will confine the eye
Of whatever being you will become,
New cage for old captive to call his home;
Once trapped by Creation's lure, you see
There is only one limit — Eternity —
Set upon life you have made your own.

A MUSIC FOR
MIDSUMMER VOICES

And pictures of a world
that begins to offer form,
meaning and tangible desires

A Music for Midsummer Voices

The night is quiet,
Darkly still.
Out of its silence voices of people
Pass beneath my windowsill—
Voices of men in slow conversation;
Voices of children
Tired and shrill;
Voices of women idly talking
Of neighbors and nonsense,
Husband and bed; voices of lovers
In concatenation
Telling what better
Were left unsaid.

So they come,
Are briefly heard,
People who loiter beneath my room,
Each reduced
To some casual word
Floated upon a summer breeze,
Reengulfed into gloom
And night-green trees
Beyond the streetlights.

*   *   *

Standing there, motionless on high,
Listening to voices
I wonder if I
Have rounded some corner of thought and time,
Configurations of a sleepless night;
Am I a summer voice,
Momentary, slight,
Partially heard upon summer air
Beneath a partly opened window where
A stranger stands
Above eternal shrubbery
In a flickering of Time's golden light?

Does some other listener
Stand unseen within his window space
High above the place I walk,
Leaning on his down-stretched hand?
Does he, too, idly note
My half-heard talk;
And does he find it idle and empty
As I pass by?
And as I pass
Are my words lost amid the choruses
Of insects in a nighttime grass?

Does he, listening, wonder idly as I do
If one will look up, idly wondering, too,
And smile perhaps,

Not seeing him at all
Within his window frame
Set in midwall
Nor understand his thought?
Or is he sure the while
That one will not?

      *   *   *

Does he then, as I,
Turn out his light,
Bend back to some sealed-off part
Of solitary need
And in the night
Study only the beating of his own heart?

Does he give no further heed
To voices that merely occupy
Emptiness, depart into silence,
Voices soon spent,
Filled with their own un-needing,
To die upon some unnecessary syllable,
Ungreiving lettering
Cut upon the porous stone
Of darkness,
Silenced, overthrown
By insect noises,
Voices vainly transitory,
Not caring to be understood;

Words meaninglessly spoken
Within a humid silence
To rise and fall and shatter
Upon summer earth
Unheard?

    *   *   *

And there, as time goes by,
Unheeded by those who come and pass
Beneath the darkened frame
Remains only emptiness of glass
Where one once stood.
Even its outline is swallowed up at last
Within the flowing black facade
Of soft black summer air.

Hours advance. Voices cease to sound.
The pulsating formlessness
Of night
Spreads along the ground,
Washes around the trunks of trees
Toward the inconceivability of dawn.

The streetlight falters, fades,
Flares up for an instant, then expires.
And in the deepest hour of darkness
At its own self-appointed, self-imagined moment,
The nothingness of night transpires . . .

Radiantly comes to be
Like a dark flower
Floating eternally fair
Upon reflective surfaces
Of voiceless summer air. . . .

Of Roses and Rue

Futile such symbols
As roses and laurel
Their beauty is faded
By a tomorrow.

Triumphant rewards
Of yesterday's winning
Are scorned and dishonored
By new need for getting.

Withered and dying
Abandoned by pride
Crowns and bouquets
Are soon cast aside.

But defeat's prize of rue
Once won by the heart
Is ever resplendent
Nor fades nor departs. . . .

Alas, later I learned
Rue drains of its sorrow,
Grows ungreen and brittle,
Has its final hour.

A hand that would hold it
Finds it, too, has clutched
Twigs whose leaves wither
And crumble to dust.

Visitation

It flew straight from eternity
Out into this night of me
To proclaim that I might once have been
Creature of pristine purity.

Child-eyed, it beat about my brain.
I raised up towers of hard gray anger
Manned by spites each armed with pain;
I marshaled troops of prejudice,
Built barricades of tangled hate,
Studied logistics of arrogance.
I clanged shut vanity's iron gate.

All this because on rapid wing
Circled through darkness self-offering,
A simple demand, a dove-like thing.

I screamed and plunged the knife of fear
When caresses seemed to touch my side;
Into the gulf of penitence
Innocence fluttered, fell and died.

The Limestone Boy

He stood at the end of the garden path,
    The Limestone Boy,
And seemed to beckon to me and laugh.
    His naked joy
Matched mine and I fell in love with him;
    I left the games,
The unsecret ways of a child of ten.
    At twenty I came

To lie at his feet in the pedestal's shade,
    To sigh and write
Verses that celebrated our love
    In erotic rhyme.
Bitter the winter when I turned thirty,
    For then I surprised
The first cold look of withdrawal
    In his stone eyes.

He is scarred by frosts, his right arm is fallen
    There in the grass.
Sitting alone in this tangle of garden
    I hear them pass,
Real boys who whistle their tunes on the street.
    But now is too late;

Harsh seasons of rust have sealed the lock
    On the garden gate;
And I am trapped here, consumed with grief
    For an image's fate.

After Autumn Harvests

This is the white autumn haze
Coming over the valley;
Days have neither beginning nor end.
Hills turn smoky brown,
As dim as painted hills,
Blend with a painted sky.
The leaves of the birch
Quake and drift toward earth
To lie as though painted in pale ochre
Upon dark ochre ground.
Through lengthening nights
The moon watches with paralyzed eye
To see where the white haze has gone.

Something rattles among the shocked corn
With a faraway sound
Like bones that dangle from a bleached bone.
A bird cries and dips from flight
As though it had flown
Into the malignance of a white spell,
As though the white haze had turned
A feathered breast
Into the intensity of plummeting stone.

Day after day the white haze comes,
Hangs low over the valley,

Tarnishes the sun,
Until I, day after day, wander aimlessly
Among the obelisks of corn
As though I had been spun
Out of the white haze —
A man without heart, viscera or soul,
Unborn — its spectral essence given form
That the white haze might
To itself become known,

That implacable coldness
Might be embodied
To prowl abroad with a stone in its hand,
Eager to smash white brains
From their sanctuary of bone,
In search of warm flesh to mangle
That blood might flow out
Upon an abandoned winter ground.

Biography of an Entrepreneur

He lived, an able man
Locked up within the room
Of his success. His toys:
The daily paper and a pile of gold,
Magazines, a television set,
And a teddy bear he cuddled in his arms at night.

He needed nothing more
To fill his life.
His blinds, half shut, admitted
Narrow slits of light
From suns he never saw.
A hamburger on a tray
He called for every day at three
And ate it drowned in catsup.

The wife, whom he had never known,
Lived in some distant room.
His children were the things his body had cast off.
When he heard them running in the corridors
He stopped his ears and coughed.

Last night he died.
Paid mourners came and broke his lock;
They carried him in slow procession,
Led by his wife and eldest son
Who wailed and named him

Through their tears;
GOOD, KIND and GENTLE,
BRAVE, GENEROUS and GOOD!

Beating their breasts and crying thus,
Over and over,
They laid him in a stone, sealed in a box,
Well locked,
To keep his spirit safe
And free them of it always.

His gold, the papers, and the teddy bear
Were given to his eldest son.
The widow locked him in the darkened room
That moral continuity might be observed.
When at three o'clock
He asked for hamburger with catsup on a tray
She knew that to perpetuity
This way of life — and with it virtue —
Would endure. Good things
For another generation
Were made secure.

Intaglio in Topaz

The polished agate sun
Sinks drowsily down;
Onyx song of bird
Disturbs an amethyst wood;
Amber shadows fade
In air's pale chrysophase.

We in the garden keep
Our appointed time;
Sunset arrows climb
Facades of light;
We meet only to part.

Hand touches hand;
You smile and stand
Silent a moment
Before you turn and go,
Serene and slow
And almost bright —
As though regret
Engraved itself upon
The shell-pink glow
Of afternoon.

. . . The departure of a faun
Across expanses
Of cypress-bordered lawn,

Sated and so
Anxious to be gone,
Yet hesitant still to go —

Reluctance perfectly defined
In the attitudes
Of antique intaglio.

Cancer — For E.G.K.

By long invalidism made ready
She lay into the pillows as though death
Were a heavy metal pumping through her veins;
Light from half-opened blinds
Scattered niggardly rays
Among inept flowers on the windowsill,
Over glasses and trays on the bedside table.
She seemed to want to talk but only smiled a little,
Moistening her lips with the spittle of her pain,
And when at last her mind
Had arranged the words it wished to say
Their tone was as flat and colorless
As the stands of yellow gray
Hair which clung about her face.
"It is not death I want
But to be done with life."
In the space between our eyes
The years like a flock of sluggish birds
Struggled up and wheeled away;
Empty girlhood evenings, waiting
Through afternoons when nothing cared to happen,
Lonely nights of which she had never spoken
Even to herself,
Tacit successions of dark silk dresses
She smoothed over her knees

As she rocked on the summer porch and listened to
Rain that fingered the roof, drained from maple leaves,
Always the same while all around her changed
Until only unfamiliar faces passed along her street;
The frame house settled eastward,
White-painted porch columns cracked and streaked,
The front steps groaned
Or would have if anyone had come up them.
Under ragged honeysuckle bushes
Surged invasions of weeds.
I forgot the cheering things I had come to say:
"Soon, very soon!" I said. Her wrist lay in my hand
Like a bird's leg, poignant,
The fingers curled like claws.
She smiled again, her lips barely moved
But no sound came. Only the eyes spoke warmly
As though my words were the first
Of commitment she had ever heard.
She died that day.

Advice to My Childhood

Run, child,
Under the light of the flaring gas lamp
Under the height of dark elm trees.
Chase, child, the girl with red hair,
Hide in trembling thickets of leaves
Beside the front porch.
Bushes are cool and secure in the night,
Untouched by spillings of too-bright light;
They are havens from grief.

Shout, child voice,
Incomprehensible meaning
Of laughter and play,
Shout the excitement of make-believing,
Make warm summer air
Momentarily gay with your throat full of sound;
Soon enough it grows still
In a new day's pale gleaming.

Breathe, child,
An odor of lilac, the moisture of grasses,
Denseness of shrubbery,
Clove-scented earth.
Deep roots are growing
And flowers are sleeping.
Wide lawns recede

Into thick hedges
Where secrets are keeping.
They will not corrupt.

Run, fast legs, in hide-and-go-seeking;
Peer, eyes, and peep
To see who is coming;
Then crouch in safe places
Away from the houses, the iron street lamp.

Let child fingers touch.

Listen, child!
The rustlings, the chirrings,
The tree toad's sharp jostlings
Are voices of warning;
Too soon comes a dawn.
Listen to yearnings
Before morning comes!

Discover the meanings,
Delicious discernings,
The furtive hand searching
Before night is done.

Libation

I drink the draft of this summer day
From springhead, honeysuckle and bee;
I imbibe its unblemished morning of light,
Its clouds that form gently and float away;
To slack longing's thirst day's sky is bright.

The purr of the water from the brook,
The perfume of a sun-heated grass
Meet and blend in sweet harmony
That sparkles into transparency
When poured together into my glass.

It is I who draw up from its willing root
The opening of the flower I pluck;
It is I who drink this crystalline hour,
Its sound, its motion and its color
Distilled for my cup by summer's ardor.

Saturday Night Dance

I am mad with dancing to the tumbling notes
That whip my weary twinkling feet.
I whirl and dance with the boys and girls,
Possessed by merry music that swirls
Out of the house and down the street.

O to escape through a windless night
Away from merriment quietly!
O to walk an unfrequented way
Beyond the village! Salt grasses sway
There on the shore of a waveless sea.

But hear! The tune has begun again;
Again I am plunged in the merry trance.
Where is my will to turn and go
To the silent place? A fiddler's bow
Scrapes its strings and I must dance.

Kaleidoscope

There was a cabinet under the stair
In my grandmother's house
Where old toys were kept.
While she slept in her big upstairs room
On a rainy afternoon
I might open the door
And take them out. . . .

They were old, not like the toys I knew.
The tumbling-clown's silk garment
Rotted, stained with mildew;
An iron bank — a donkey
Kicked pennies into a box —
Was rust and scarred paint. The lock
On the pencil box with lacquer flamingoes
Was broken.

             All those things were forgotten
When I found the kaleidoscope.
It was a paper tube with one ground-glass end
And opposite that a lens
Which you put to your eye.
When you turned it there would begin
Change, an infinite sequence of patterns
Made from reflections on fixed mirrors within
Formed and reformed always, I knew,

Out of the same fragments of colored glass
Sealed into the far end of the black tube.

As rain fell out of doors
I would sit on the floor under the stairs
And view red, yellow, green and blue
Shift and return to a combination
They had not had before;
A compelling game,
Better than any you played
With a board and dice, always new
Yet always almost the same,
The red sometimes falling against green,
Sometimes against yellow,
And sometime resting again upon the blue.

That is when I must have learned, I think,
Something of why patterns changed:
You turn the tube the very least bit
And all of its elements
Will suddenly rearrange.

Something of what forms patterns:
Just a few pieces of colored glass,
Yellow and green, red and blue,
Multiplied by mirrors placed out of view
In a black tube

So that new arrangements of color grew
Continuously in front of your eye.

Something of how engrossing patterns can be:
They were never the same
— Or could they be,
Revolve the tube long enough?
A whole hour might pass away
As I turned the kaleidoscope
And I had forgotten everything —
Grandmother, other toys, closed-in day.

Something, too, of what patterns are all about —
Green and yellow, blue and red,
Yellow and blue, yellow and green, green and blue,
Yellow, blue, green, red —
Whenever a new pattern was formed
An old pattern disappeared; a pattern was dead —
Or had it only gone into some place
From which it might return?

. . . A mystery for a rainy afternoon
While grandmother slept,
Something colorful to do on a long afternoon
When the sun was temporarily hidden from view
And the day was cold and gray and wet.

. . .To a Remembered Child

Sit, child, small in imagining's room
Furnitured with encircling gloom;
Stare at the future as you used to do;
Stare at me, as I stare at you.

Unsuspected pattern links our eyes;
I see the emerging shapes of fear
That you made yours. Do you hear my sighs?
I taste your uncomprehended tear.
Child, look at me! Do you recognize
Some part of you surviving our years;
Am I any man you are glad to see?

You stop your reading, rise and go
To the luminous square of fading window.
Familiar darkness settles down
Over the street and an eveninged lawn.
I feel your hand as it touches the pane;
I see you listening through the dark
To children at play beneath the elms;
You turn away and close your book.
Dear child, was I standing beneath those trees,
A shadow already shadowed by leaves?

Around you a silent house grows chill.
You dejectedly lean on the windowsill;

Mahogany chairs; the copper lamp
Gleams about you in the damp
Of summertime dusk. Do you mourn the still
Frail hand of death which set them thus,
That ran so light on piano keys,
Or tumbled pale hair as you sat on her knee?
Everywhere within the house
Loneliness echoes, ominous.

Alas, poor child, how can I know
What longings of mine to your longing eyes show?
Are you mystified by what you see —
This antique room in gilded light,
The tasselled draperies long and white,
Tapestried benches against the wall,
What do they signify to you?
Does a fulfilled hope here meet your eye
Or a heart of desirous complexity?
But what can we understand of these?

Lonely child, if in me your need
To love and be loved could be satisfied,
Then what love you gave, with hope without pride,
Might be recompensed by what love I seek.

What of peace might we both not find
Beyond custom's well-schooled futilities

In each others arms? Could an atonement
By bitter-shared tears bring us at-onement?

Though we cling close, how can I relearn
What innocent seeking your thoughts intern;
How, my child, can I realize
Such mysteries of change as entwine our eyes,
That by more than space and time must ban
The man from the child, the child from the man?

Farewell, child, I shall not come again
To see immature pain or show it my own.
I leave you to taste your grief alone,
Remain here in the future, your unknown room.
Why must you know where a longing must lead?
Be content, pale child, beneath summer trees.

An Exaltation

I reeled, and borne on fiery wings
Summited a universe.
I walked beneath a canopy of kings
Into a large surrounding land
Paved with gold, with petal, with pearl,
Lit by the flaming of a terrible jewel;
Watered by a flowing from the font of Time.

All around me, soundlessly heard,
Rushed the mummer of contented good.
I bore the weight of prodigious light,
I felt a joyous laughing boy
Go nakedly across my sight,
I saw a manifold happy cry
Go out from sea and star and sky.

When on languid wing I sank
Back into a bosoming world
And plunged to slumber, I clean forgot
Where I had gone, what I had heard.
Yet lying here with limbs all curled
I trembled still with what I was
And, waking, knew what I was not.

Lines Concerning His Desk

He came into the room, sat down at it,
And knew immediately that it was haughtily aloof
Because it failed to cover his knees at once.
Speaking to it kindly, firmly, he rebuked
The way it stared at him with a glossy look.
He pounded on its flat and oblong top.
And it said thump. He twisted it by one ugly leg
Until with a splintering sound it broke.

The contents of its drawer he dumped upon the floor,
Where things lay staring back — pencils, photographs,
Blotters, erasers, unpaid bills all jumbled from its lap.
He cursed its regularity of line with nasty words,
Its cubic style; humbled and berated it
With vile and obscene gestures, obtuse smirks
Which implied the impotence of varnish, screws,
Polished surfaces and decorative grooves.

But there it stood, tipsy and broken leg'd,
Its drawer removed, and regarded him superiorly
Quite unmoved, with a sort of passive criticism
That rejected every aspect of his uncalled-for mood,
His fleshly human softnesses; his desk, all his,
Waiting to serve him whenever he should choose.

On the Demands of the Sublime

A thousand verses
Have been writ on Helen's face (or,
Hers being esteemed the very face of beauty,
Likely more); on the blossoming of an apple tree in spring;
On the ferocity of the Afric lion's roar.
So why do I strive to revive this war with words once more?

I cannot answer
For the pulchritude of Helen's face
Or for the majesty with which a lion speaks,
But the blooming of an apple tree after a rain-filled night
Explodes its blossoms in my throat
And sends forth verbal legions of my spring.

I suppose
A searcher after Helen's ravishment
Would never tire of dithyrambs designed to set afire
His Trojan quest. I'm told some blacks
Who hunt the lion through sun-heavy grass
Must sit at dusk around a fire of spears
And chant the glory of his lordship's name,
The yellow of his eyes, the craftiness of his paws,
The trophy of his mane. . . .

For it must always be
That as long as tentacles of a man reach out

To take some grasp of what he needs but lacks means for,
There will be those who speak by the armament of metaphor
To take up the attack; so warriors who will listen raptly
To another verse on Helen's golden hair,
To chant the way the lion springs upon its prey,
To versify on how apple blossoms cast their scent
Into morning air to impel a day
Toward some victory that had not been before . . .

At least as long as we
Have not become so worldly wise
That there is no longer anything to say,
Beyond newspaper formulas of prose,
To glorify the invitation of Helen's eyes.

Circus, Circus

1.

When it comes time
To give up the remembered past
I'll let go last
That first circus parade I saw;

The gilded carriages, the cage
Of monkeys rolling along
A summer street, tasselled stallions
Prancing in the shade of maple trees,

Red band uniforms with gold braid
(The calliope made high leaves shake!)
And all the rest that only one
Chasing chariots in the sun

Of decades younger could have known.
Racing breathlessly beside
The bedizened elephants
Is the only time that I can recall

Forgetting everything, all
Of what I had so far touched or seen.
I became excitement itself —
Splendor, motion, sound made manifest

Somehow, through whole festivals
Of childish eyes recklessly endowed

With a mile of glittering opportunity
To see. Only to see! To see! To see!

2.
The monkeys
Jabber, jabber, jabber
All day long
Within their cage
As though to justify
To each other
The pleasures
Of their unclean ways.

3.
He walks upon the wire
Nor seems to care at all
For space which violently attends
The terror of a fall.

He moves at ease nor hesitates,
Supreme in spangled tights,
To accept taut isolation
Decreed by glaring lights.

He walks upon the wire
As though no one were there;
With only a tender smile he baits
The netlessness of air,

While below him ignored humanity
Shines toward his feet
And experiences, chameleon-like,
Nobility from his deed

Nor guesses that his serenity
Which holds the whole tent still
Is but the sum of all its fears
Bound tightly by his will.

4.
The lion frames his face with fury,
Strides his bars with arrogance
And in the spotlight of the ring
Spits and strikes when forced to dance.

He leaps upon the high-set stool,
Compelled by curtly gesturing whip,
And snarls, for he has come to know
The mystery of its stinging tip.

Only later, when the tent grows still,
Does he within his shuttered cage
Lick his paws and purr and wonder
The uselessness of a lion's rage.

5.

If you have not seen
The fat woman in the sideshow
You cannot know
How what is human
Can become obscene;
Extruded from itself
Into fold upon fold
Of flesh or something spongy,
Like desire or fear,
In which decay is carefully concealed
And where a greenish gray mold
Grows in oily crevices
Out of the light of day.

She leaned over the rail
And I could just barely hear her say,
"Get me something cool to drink, dearie,
It's so hot in here."
But when the whole mass of fat seemed to lean
Toward me
In a convulsive, hesitating way,
I turned and ran fast
To get out of there,
Afraid.

A VOYAGE

And other pieces of an
introspective nature

A Voyage — Upon Open Waters

1.
This sea is wide,
Extends itself beyond
The meager dimension of thought.

Shore, moved away,
Drops downward out of sight
Into the interstices of eternity
Which ring horizon's curve.
The dome of sky
Rests quietly upon the surface of the waters
And centers me
Within circumference.

2.
How long, how long!
Hours, leagues; what measurements
Since I, a landsman always,
Living at a pretty coastal place
And oriented by the meeting line of shore and sea,
Resolved to trust this boat and sail away?

When locked within a circle
Time's boundaries merge
And its demarcations are erased.

What impulse moved me to embark?

The waterfront was still;
I was alone.

The circuit of mind,
Seeking a source,
Returns into itself;
Beginning is formed within the act,
And cause springs from its own accomplishment.

The planks and pilings of the wharf
Were gilded by an early sun.
I walked until I reached the end,
Dropped down into this open boat,
Loosened the rope
And fell away to sea.

When did I pass beyond the sight of land?
Precisely at what moment was I borne
From familiar shallow water
Bounded by a shore
Into this deep of sky and sea
And sunlit surge which circumscribes my boat?

Time becomes supple, loses reference points
When bent into animated arcs of experience.
Moment to moment flows,
Assumes sequence,
Fuses one circle out of all.

3.

At noon a bird entered the canopy of sky,
Circled my boat close in,
Veered sharply toward the sun,
Swerved, and I watched him dart
A multi-angled course
Aimed into the very center of the sky —
Where he and I met headlong
And, suddenly made one, were absorbed and lost
In the blue nucleus of infinity.

Past and future
When sufficiently compressed
Fuse, lose identity
To form the precarious substance
Of the present,
The dangerous
And irreversible potential of now.

Time burst!

Sky melted into sea,
Released, ran down in rivulets;
And sea, released,
O'erflowed the upward limit of the sky,
Poured in, turned liquid light,
And streaming, drenched the sun.

Space, freed of Time

And become immediate, begins to flow,
Releases boundaries
And moves, escapes its edges,
Expands, flows thin,
Engulfs the mind and spirit,
Encompasses their spaces within itself
And is by them absorbed.

A sun descended, tide altered flow,
The sky and sea returned each to its sphere,
Met once again to form horizon.
I turned my boat and pointed it toward shore.

4.
Within the shrinking circle of water and air
I float upon the body of the wave,
I move with its direction,
Yet never seem to move at all,
Nor have a direction of my own,
But always center on myself
All sea and sky.

There is a larger dimension
Unrelated to a line of shore.

Ceaseless tensions
Bear upward underneath my boat,
Lift it, propel it on,

While I remain motionless
And all that surrounds me moves.

There are forces
Not resolved upon a beach.

5.
Ahead the escarpment of the town appears
Above its walls and wharves
Within its quadrant of the sea.
It draws an irregular shadow
Along the narrow sand where water
Overflows the land
To etch its silver line
Against all encroachment of the deep.

A woman looks along the beach,
Waves, beckons up its length
To one she loves.
A man runs down
To reach the water's edge,
Swims naked within the breaking surf
From which his immediacy is formed.

All movement takes place
Upon its own appointed sheet of Time.

Children play in pools,

Choose shells, build castles
Of wet sand
Within their dimensionless transparency
Of hour and place and light.

There is a plane of act
Where that begins
Which surfaces the void.

6.
I, who once have sailed
Upon the boundless sea,
Timeless and immeasurably deep,
Return;
To tell you that your line of beach
Is only a stopping place for thought.
Preceding it lies beginning.
It is the sea which signifies your land.

And when a man,
Adrift in an open boat,
Is cleaved by bird and centered in sunlight
He learns, within an instant
No larger than a mustard seed,
To orient himself anew.

That which is oriented
Balances upon a point,
Stable, yet of the essence

Of all precariousness,
Being poised upon a center which is not there,
Yet which there does exist,
Where forces meet
And by their meeting
Annul themselves
Wherefrom mirroring tensions
Surge forth to crest and break
And by their retreat toward the center
Lift to crest and break, and crest again
Until they reach a shore that is not there,
Thereby to become visible at last;
To spread and sink and die
Upon the impermanence of a beach.

7.
Perhaps
The essence of the sea is this;
Whichever way
A man may turn his boat
The distance to his horizons
Remains unchanged;
Whether he may row or not,
Toward whatever compass point,
His center and the center of the sea
Will stay the same.
His mystery becomes

The mystery of the sea,
The reason why the sea exists
And why when adrift upon it
In an open boat, cleaved
By a bird and light,
He may experience
(And partially understand?)
Something of the unique enigma
Of himself
And the sequences of event,
The interlocking circles of being,
By which Time inscribes life
Upon Its own Eternity.

Wintered City

Into the city
Soft snow drifts
As ashes of bone might if
The bones having died
Were ground fine cast aside
Back into the streets
In which they had lived
To float downward through air
Frost filled debonair
And slowly seal earth
Until silence extends
Through the town where an end
Has come to stone tongues
Reserves of dark cold
Have caught hold
The city is dumb
Strangled by snow
No buses trucks go
Store fronts are like
Old askew monuments
Whose epitaphs show
In archaic neon glow
Where a city has been
High in windows are lights
World and wealth can resume

When a pale winter sun
Will reanimate sky
Now the city lies white
In snow drifts of night
And remembers in sleep
In the dream in the brief
Recall of lost time
That its weakness has grown
That its limits are known
That a wind   a red flower
Or summery silences
Earthquake or shower
Still could take over
Dismantle the power
Prided by men
That the unknown has set
And remembers the hour
When cities began
And when cities will end

Patterns on an Autumn Afternoon

I walk along the woodland road,
    An autumn way leaf-carpeted,
      Where bare branch leans above my head.
I prance and leap and caracole
    Through crackling heaps of brown and red.
Strewn about an ancient bole
The acorns, firm and capped and whole,
    Assure gray squirrels of winter feast.
A breeze bounds lightly from a knoll
    Beyond the wood, while from the east
    The sun springs forth, an innocent beast
Like leopard cub with spotted coat
    Who gambols among the trees. A least
Late greenness warms the southern slope
Of pastureland as though some hope
    Of growing there refused to sleep.
Grapevines cast their twisted rope
    Between the trunks of birches to keep
    Them linked throughout the deep
Assault of winter in comradeship.

    Above my freedom wide skies sweep
Behind bare branches. White clouds skip
As do my thoughts.
              Unwarned I dip
    From carefree elation to despair;

Autumn gaieties from me slip.
  Broken the summer beyond repair!
  It is winter's threat which fills the air;
All living is doomed to grief. I stand
  Beside the pasture fence and there
In shivering sunlight I understand
How sorrow surprises a joyous land.

Moon Dance

That night the moon shone down on me
Through clouds. Its whiteness grew
Into an eye which peered through lids
Stained with bloody dew.

I crouched and crept, it searched me out,
A hand relentlessly pressed
Downward until silver claws
Could search within my breast.

Something secret leapt from me,
With terror I was torn.
I fear myself; I fear the sun;
I hide away from morn

Drained of some essential part
Sucked up by moon's cold flame —
An emptiness so dreadful
I dare not know its name.

But I come forth when moon shines bright
And dance because I know
That in its light I can worship myself
Made free from all here below.

On the Lake Front

The negro boy
With dark face smiling
Walks along the waterfront
And casts a pebble
In the lake
Just to hear its pleasant plunk.

The negro boy
Walks by the water,
Kicks the sand
With ragged toe.
Behind him, rising
Terrace on tower,
Stone flowers of a city grow.

The negro boy
Casts forth his pebble
To the brightness
Of the lake,
But never hears
Its pleasant sound
Above the clatter a city makes,

Except within
His unsmiling mind
Where, when he casts
The pebble, a plunk

Clearly rises
From dark slow circles
Where its counterpart
Has sunk.

Stallionesque

A white stallion ranges
The forested hills —
His mane and his tail are like iced water flowing;
His eyes are terrifyingly still.
I have seen him alone
In a circle of trees
Pawing the earth;
He was shrill with unease
And arched his neck. Often at dusk
He comes to the wire of this lowland pasture,
Driven down by an incandescent lust.
He breaks the rest of the tame mares
Who raise their heads and start —
Rise and wheel wildly along the fence
And whinny amorously in a gathering dark.

Painting in Grissaile

Endlessly rain runs down
From a shut sky.
Across the street the trees
Seem torn from dirty paper.
They lean forward to meet
Above streaming lawns and nullify
Day's meaning
With leaves down drooping.

A man with stooping shoulders,
As thin as a ghost,
Walks close
Against a wall,
He presses under the eaves,
Gray through the mist,
Not real at all.

Drip, drop, drip, drop.

Endlessly rain falls
From the closed sky
And in this closed room I
Wait endlessly, endlessly call
Upon the rain to stop.

Advice to the Past

Leave the shadows at rest,
Let them lay
In their grave on the ground
Undisturbed;
Let old songs fade on the wind,
Borne away, no more sung
No more heard.

Mourn no more the fate
Of the moth which has entered
Its brightness of flame
Nor seek to recall
Those dim figures
Fled down Time's path:
They will not come again.

Be contented that all things end,
That a night will follow each day;
Let be whatever has been,
Let flow smoothly and cleanly away
Old joy and old pain which when held
Weight the hand,
Make its gestures unsure;
The small daily part
Of Time's burden is more
Than what is not Divine
Can endure.

Untitled

They were alone that night within the house.
Her husband had been gone almost a week
Absent on business at the county seat.
The boy awoke, wondering at first,
Listening to the pad of stealthy feet
That came into his room
From cold sleep-weighted night.
He was nineteen, he earned his board and keep
By doing chores about the place.
He had a pleasant face, a slight
And graceful body, different from his,
Her husband's, made stalwart and ugly
By the work around the farm.
He knew that she had eyed him occasionally,
Watching him move but meaning, then, no harm.

Afterward, he felt her sated body lift,
Thinking him fast asleep. Breathing heavily
She crawled from the tangled bed and left his side.
He lay there, clenched and hidden in the dark,
And cried.

After the Theatre

Like the prescient unfolding
Of an amber bloom,
Soft fronding of lamplight
Spreads within the room;

From darkly mirrored streets
Beyond the windowpane
Yellow buds of lamplight
Burst through rain.

We enter, she throws her furs
Onto the nearest chair,
Turns, poses, lifts her hand
Woman-like against her hair.

Speaks sharply, "I am not jealous!"
Then the fears,
Guarded so long behind her eyes,
Crystallize into tears.

Her foot stamped on the floor
Echoes, sharpening
The quiet of the room. She continues:
"It is so disheartening

"The way you neglect me,
Oh, only as a friend.

What of the little necessary things,
Where does a friendship end

"And something less begin?
I know your heart
Has no space meant for me,
I know that part.

"Confess, you would use
And delicately cast aside!
Oh, when will you understand
That I, a woman, I have pride

"And pride gets hurt, even a woman's!
It is only now and then
When nerves are taut
That — that one is hurt again."

I light her cigarette
With desperate motion,
Striving to make the match flame
Signify emotion.

Darkly the figure of our lifted hands
Reflected on the windowpane
Mingles with the streetlights
Quenched in rain.

A Drawing of a Departure

There
Back in the gloom
At the end of the passage
Lies the room
Where the boy dies.

Mute
In filtered light
Like water over golden sand
His chair, his table,
His books stand,
Ordered so by his own hand;
In the closet
Shadowy folds of garments hang.

Below
The half-drawn blind
Insects hum above the grass;
Flowers bend in a south wind
Along the path.

Beyond
The hedge
People loiter along the walk,
Stare idly at the white house,
Idly talk.

While he,
Borne beyond sound or touch,
Draped in sheets upon a narrow bed
Stretches out his hand as though to reach
The ceiling overhead
Where light-shadows dance,

Brightness
Reflected from medicine
In a water glass,
As though some image had withdrawn
To just beyond the searching of his fingertips,
And hovered there where it had flown
Directly above his eyes,
That it might cast one
Backward glance upon
An already relinquished form,

Hesitant
At the last moment to go,
Yet definitely anxious
To be gone.

Measurement

Bright steel shaft of ultimate longitude
Triangles angles mystic hexagonal symbols
Oh Zero plus O + nothing
Equals infinitude
Curves long-lifting to perilous arcs
Curving of light and curving of sound
And curving of time
Set the space of the soul
In invisible unbroken unparallel nonextant lines
Immeasurability measured
Awful exactitude
2 x 2 is forever

PARAGRAPHS

Brief introspections, images
and episodes extracted
from the flow of Time

Paragraphs

1.

Snowflakes feather the window ledge,
Muffle a darkening windowpane;
The dormant bleakness of branch and hedge
Stirs in soft dreams of blossoming.

Houses familiar across the way
Blur and dissolve; drifting veils of white
Isolate an end of day,
Enclose the room in a cold twilight

Beyond any light that is touched by Time.
Forgotten the book, remote the moment;
Then the lamp — around me shines
A golden network of the present.

2.

Loneliness wells up from the heart
Like oasis water from sand
To form a trembling crystal spring
Among drifting dunes of mind.

Stoop, unafraid, to drink from it;
By loneliness be refreshed;
Its ever-flowing purity
Of all liquors is the best;

Alone can quench a bitter need,
Assuage the dusty thirst
Of one who has traveled long across
Time's parched and unmapped wastes.

3.
The broken twisted bush is the only one that dares
To put a flower forth in the hostile winter hush;
The broken twisted bush does not blossom unaware
Of cold danger from the north, poised inclemency of air;
The broken twisted bush grows, intent upon a need
To give extravagance from itself, reasoning neither
      sap nor seed;
The broken twisted bush will succumb before the
      spring,
Self-generated sacrifice to unmundane blossoming;
The broken twisted bush out-examples winter's power
By the simplicity of its daring — one unblemished
      frozen flower.

4.
Blessed be those who
Have paid off the mortgage

Blessed be those who
Have enough gas for the Cadillac

Blessed be those who

Have cast their steaks
Onto the barbecue grill

Blessed be those
Pass the barbecue sauce
Blessed
Please pass the Bromo Seltzer
In thy name
Forever and ever

Amen

5.
The real needs of the body are so few
After its superficial needs have been shed;
There is nothing the body really needs to do
But lie on its back and let sunlight stain closed lids red.

The needs of the mind are not the needs it thinks.
It best spends long unheralded hours
Silently staring with never an eyelid's blink
At ants in the grass, or imagining faces on flowers.

The needs of the soul are simple,
Uncomplicated by any theologies.
Reasonless, it can leap with joy, turn nimble
Or consume itself in an autumn bonfire of leaves.

The needs of death are the purest needs of all —

A summer night's yearning with eagerness drained away
When the limited notes of the whip-poor-will,
Reiterated in darkness, overpower the ear.

6.

I have had a thousand lives,
A thousand deaths;
A hundred successes,
A hundred failures;
Ten loves and ten hates;
Now I go in search of myself.

7.

Upon a smaller orbit I move, withal, at ease,
Nor do those spaces I have left, my new dimension tease;
It is not distance makes a curve but movement of a kind;
The character of circling to circles is confined.
A place worth any reaching upon unmeasured path
By limiting grows possible, a reasoned infinite;
And anything worth grasping along a boundless rim
Is had with more aplombness in what a hand can span.
What is lost of far and wide by a constricted round
Enlarges to new dimension: contrasts of up and down.

8.

Angry fiend within my heart,
Do not despair, do not depart;

My anger endure who anger preaches;
Anger endured patience teaches;
Patience learned by you or by me
Assures that neither shall angered be.
Stay, incite me to acts of danger
Designed to castigate dangerous anger;
When me you goad to tranquility
You shall, my friend, serene spirit be.

9.
At night the stars, their multitude beyond compare;
Stars and stars and stars — stars everywhere!
Bladed beyond the scope of eye, green spears of grass
In pastures infinite beneath the feet!
Such vasts of knowledge that confront the single mind,
How weak are estimates, how humankind!

10.
Once I removed neatly plates and suet and bone
From the table whereon I ate,
But then I had not learned eating alone.
Now I make feeding's closed place
By just shoving away the gnawed debris of the past.
I find such to be a most sensible way, more convenient, too,
In spite of what etiquette's treatises say
A civilized man should do.

11.

To secrete nectar, store it up
Between the two it matters not:
The sugary suck of root, or probe
Of sipper is the work — the pact
Where bee and flower together partake
One meaning from conjunctive act,
By wing or color participate
In sequences of honey's pact.
Neither shall divorce the other,
Flower from bee or bee from flower;
The honey only stands alone,
One nectarous yellow in waxen comb.

12.

Moth within whose flame does dwell
Total encompassment of hell,
Fly on to enter your fiery tent
And there fold wings consumed, content
That you have achieved as few others may
The holocaust of your destiny.

13.

Grass grows thick on the ground
Blade touching blade forever;
Pigeons roost under the eave
Feather to feather.

Men alone are like stars,
Isolate, burning and bright,
Bound away from each other
By spaces of night.

14.

I have been mostly as a gnat
Darting forth and whining back
In random circles which accomplish
Little worthy of finer polish;

Now I would shellfish become
And work upon one spiralled home
Washed randomly, a timeless shell
Constructed carefully of pearl.

15.
The night sky is as pale as swamp water
And I am filled with unrest;
The sound of insects among grasses stirs the foreground
Of consciousness with insistent request.
A full moon extends fingers of light
To probe white-skinned hills that lie naked
Along the horizon. Finite stars that pit
The bloodless sky are the scars of wounds
Which cannot heal until fires of night die down
And dawn with unbright hands erases the lesions of unquiet.

16.

Wild sunflowers thrust flat blossoms out
To every side from wirey stalks;

Weaving their flight among sunflower flowers
Canaries skim, twirl, dart and hover,

Perch on stiff stems and sway yellow discs,
Fly away lost among dangerous bursts;

Road and sky crumble, exploded into
Instants of yellow, yellow, yellow!

17.

Poetry is that exercise
By which the fledgling spirit flies
Beyond pedestrian definition
Of words to heights of intuition.

Learning so to be borne aloft
Spirit loses earth as mounting hawk,
Attains blue realms of native yonder,
Lost to all but soaring's wonder.

Joyous, it courses a wordless chasm
Borne on currents of mysticism,
Glides through silent mystery
Where wing lies still on ecstasy.

18.

Does the ox before the blow is given
Know a bitterness toward heaven,
Tree unleaved by winter's wind
Deplore the inconstancy of spring?

Does grass when trodden lie and weep,
A flower when plucked succumb to grief,
The dove beneath the falcon's spur
To pangs of its destiny demur?

It is man alone who must divide
Sweet from bitter, enamored of good,
And so by theologies deny
That Divine impartiality is love.

19.

Fool, fool, fool!
Is all that I can sing,
To think that one still young can miss
The restlessness of spring.

Fool, fool, fool
To think that one could pass
Heedless through a leaping time
And greening of the grass.

Fool, fool, fool!
He lives in vain who dies

Without snowdrop and hepatica
Sought and idolized.

Fool, fool, fool!
Who counts the calendar days
To button a winter coat against
The sun's first ardent rays.

20.
The truth of me
Is not this tree
So richly leaved
On a summer's day.

Only branches bright
With wintry light
Bare and bereaved
True form display.

21.
April is a leaping month;
The wintered heart turned suitor
Finds the glance of tender days
Still rare among the bitter.

April is a teasing month;
The heart is tempted sorely
To forever foreswear a coy
Caress that warms so slowly.

April is a testing month;
The heart must await the day
Of nubile metamorphosis
To the willingness of May.

22.

Gone are old angers, envy is dead,
Departed are vanities, cold wings outspread;
Dark plagues of fear, vanquished, have fled;
This house stands empty of scurrilous dreads.

Now shall contentment herein be found
And joyousness fill pristine rooms with sound,
Troupes of new praises shall romp on the lawn —
Throw open closed shutters, let light abound!

23.

I walk on the hills
And a young wind pushes
Fingers through my hair;
Bracken bows down,
Clouds break apart,
Leaves tremble in rain-soaked air.

Trees green and blue
Look out from a mist
Like the figures in a frieze.
The sun bursts forth,

I shout for joy
And leap on the hills and dance!

24.

God strides forth and heavens ring,
Saints cry loudly for suffering,
Men swarm earth eager and shrill;
I shall walk over this wooded hill
In an afternoon quiet of trembling leaves;
I shall be idle beneath these trees!

25.

To me some days,
Seated on my porch,
My hills are small and green —
On others bare and large

Scaled to what
That moment I am become,
A singularly serene,
A neglected small old man.

But on another day,
Dejected and alone,
I view the sunny hills
And contentment from them flows.

How am I to define

Counterpoises of change
Between the hills and me,
The power of hills to gauge?

26.
I will hide my Poetry under the Rock
In the Pasture of my own Mind,
Where you, my Brother, shall in Yourself,
The Self I have hidden, there find.

ABOUT
THE AUTHOR

Frank Beidler Cornell (1909–2001) was born in Oak Park, Illinois. Upon completing studies at Chicago's New Trier High School, he entered Dartmouth College, where he majored in English and was graduated in 1931 with cum laude rank and as a member of the Phi Beta Kappa national honor society. ¶ Following a period he spent in the ranch country of South Dakota during the depths of the Great Depression of the 1930s, he returned to Chicago and entered upon a business career, initially with a major general-wholesaling company, prior to his establishing, as its co-proprietor, a package-design firm there. ¶ During the Second World War, he served (1942–1945) as an Intelligence officer with the United States Navy, principally in the Pacific theatre of operations, rising to the rank of Lieutenant Commander. ¶ In the course of the post-war era, he disengaged from business and turned special attention to the remodeling of a town house in one of Chicago's architecturally historic areas and, later, to the renovation of a farmhouse in central Wisconsin. While thus engaged and ongoingly until the close of his life, he particularly devoted himself to the writing of poetry, which had been for him a central pursuit from his early years, and also to the arrangement of his overall body of poetic output, in preparation for its intended multi-volume publication, posthumously, as *Poems from A House of Glass*.

INDEXES OF
POEM TITLES
AND FIRST LINES

Index of Poem Titles

Index of First Lines